Real Estate Agent 2.0

The Six Figure Success Formula Of Selling Real Estate Like It's Nothing

I0482245

Table of Contents

Conclusion

Introduction

Selling real estate is a really profitable venture. The commissions from every successful sale coupled with the high fine life that being a real estate agent entails is truly an attractive one. But let not this lure you into believing that every real estate agent lives that kind of life. The truth is that the path to success in every facet of the real estate realtor universe is a littered one. It is littered with failures; ambitious folk who started with quite the amount of motivation and psyche, but never quite managed to make a living out of it.

It is one thing to be ambitious when venturing into real estate and is a completely different thing to transition from being a complete beginner real estate agent to a pro who everyone wants to deal with. Being a successful real estate agent is a lot more than knowing someone is selling a home, finding a buyer, picking up keys to the house, opening the house for the potential buyer, making a few phone calls to negotiate the price and getting paid a commission. So, what is it that makes a successful real estate agent? What is it that makes the difference between the real estate agent of today and the real estate agent of the 60s and 70s? Or should you just use the same old strategies that the agents of the 60s and 70s were using? Well, certainly, you need to embrace the changes that have taken place over the years while ensuring that you maintain some of the good traits that made real estate agents of the past to be successful. If you are struggling with breaking into the real estate agent business world, let this book mark the end of your struggle because it will teach you actionable strategies on how to get started, build a name for yourself and remain at the top while ensuring that you attract a stream of customers with so much ease.

You can be sure that you won't have to count on luck to succeed as a real estate agent when you implement the strategies that this book will teach you.

Thanks again for downloading this book, I hope you enjoy it!

Chapter 1: Getting Started

Delving into, and selling real estate be it by use of technology as the main platform or otherwise is a broad topic by all means and it comes with multiple subtopics that often differ greatly from each other. You have residential, office, industrial, retails, recreational, agricultural, schools, raw land, hospitals, schools, parking lots etc under the broad topical umbrella. As a rule, you must pick one of these as your specialty and keep a conscious knowledge of the rest. The other thing you may not know is that each is so specialized and compartmentalized that it will be anything but easy to work up expertise in more than just one.

If you take up the task of going through the multiple "getting started as a real estate agent" articles, pieces and blogs out there, the needless technical junk eventually does a great job of putting you off real estate especially as a realtor novice. While it is true that there are indeed technical paths to bridge before you can make a dime off the field, eventually, the deal closer is property changing hands. This chapter, rather than take the obvious route and try to sound intelligent (at the expense of your understanding as a realtor), will ease you into straightforward ways that are important as you get started and serve to prepare you for the Real Estate Agent 2.0 concept.

The first step to take is stack up your realtor knowledge base. Technology or no technology, you will make a sorry realtor if your knowledge tank only has dregs to it. So, how can you learn the nuts and bolts in real estate so that you can use what you've learnt to make it big in the industry? Well, although "how to" books in real estate are a great starting point, they might not give you industry specific ideas and strategies on what to do when faced with different situations. You can think of it in the same lines that employers think of fresh graduates; they always say that graduates are half baked and not really prepared for the real world because what you learn in class (and in books) is much about theory but not the actual practice. It is only when you are knowledgeable, experienced, and passionate when you can actually offer all the needed reassurance and handholding to your clients to keep them put throughout the transaction. This simply means one thing; although you can leverage on technology to generate leads, the ball is ultimately on your side as far as closing a deal is concerned. This calls for you to learn the art of closing, which you can only learn from others unless you want to learn from yourself by making costly mistakes in the beginning. So, where do you get this industry specific knowledge?

Well, the number one source of real estate realtor knowledge is from the practicing realtors who have been successful in the industry. And where do you get these successful real estate agents? Obviously, you don't find these everywhere; these are the big shots in the industry who probably handle big money real estate transactions without having sleepless nights about it. Well, before you can know where to find these, perhaps it is necessary to determine your path as a real estate agent because this will probably be the first step towards determining where you will find the successful real estate agents.

Route #1: Follow the apprentice route

One of the ways to get started into the world of being a real estate agent is to start as a sales assistant for a recognized agent in your neighborhood. But this calls that you be a person who can follow directions/orders, and can get tasks done without being followed. Since the established agent will probably have more work than he or she can handle, be prepared to work at odd hours because being a real estate agent will need a lot of that even as you advance your skills level and grow in reputation. As such, it is important to be aware that this is really not the kind of route that anyone would follow especially given the demanding nature of the work schedules. Many agent assistants often start their own real estate agent businesses several years after working for the established agents. Nonetheless, this can catapult you to start off your own real estate agency on a better footing compared to if you opted to go it on your own from the beginning. But before you can start off, it is important to ensure that you sign all the necessary documents relating to the terms of the agreement as you work as an independent contractor and not an employee to the established agent.

You should agree on the monthly stipend and how much of the agent's commission you will earn for each completed sale (this is often between 5-10percent of the agent's net commission in the beginning although this amount is likely to increase with time). You should also ensure that you agree on how much commission you will receive for each new client you bring to the business (this could range between 25-35%) of the lead agent's net commission depending on the level of guidance and oversight you will need throughout the transaction. However, this could increase to 40-50% in later years.

So, why should you work with a successful apprentice when you could start on your own and pocket all the commissions?

Well, for starters, a successful agent can mentor you thoroughly such that you can be very knowledgeable on the ins and outs of real estate transactions within a really short time (normally within 2 years as opposed to 10-15 years if you were to do it alone). Additionally, when you work for a successful real estate agent, you are assured that you can be part of or even observe some large high end and often complex real estate transactions that you really wouldn't have gotten as a rookie real estate agent.

In addition, as an established real estate agent is mentoring you, you will have an opportunity to mix and interact with the who is who in the real estate business (buyers, sellers, contractors, attorneys, architects etc). This is certainly a great way to make more than if you start your own business finding affordable rentals for neighbors and college roommates etc. And in some instances, you might even be surprised that you might end up developing great chemistry that could lead to a partnership down the road.

Path #2: Real estate developer office

If you need a salary to help you get started, then working for an established real estate developer is a great way to start off as a real estate agent. If you start at the sales office, you will probably be at the center of many of the meetings relating to real estate transactions, which means that you can learn a lot from your position. The downside of this route is that you might need to constantly repeat the sales pitches since these have already been set so all you have to do is to repeat them to the prospective buyers.

Path #3: Other beginnings

If you cannot afford to go through the first path above due to time constraints or other commitments, this doesn't mean that you cannot start off your career as a real estate agent. For instance, you could visit different real estate agencies around your area then try to observe how the transactions are being conducted, how the agents talk to prospective buyers and property owners etc. This will probably teach you a thing or two about negotiations in real estate and you will find the skills you learn here very helpful for years to come by.

To add on, you will realize that real estate agents seem to know the areas that they sell property in and out. As such, you need to know your "sphere of influence" fully so that you can know where literally everything is and the names of different houses. This means that you ought to drive around and check out as many open houses as possible then ensure that you make as many contacts as possible. This doesn't mean that you have to start making new contacts; simply leverage on the networks you already have to spread the word about what you do. In some instances, you might need to seek help from an experienced realtor to help you close a deal even if it means you paying him or her half of the commission especially if you are starting your own business.

Path #4: Going it alone in business

This is as simple as the name suggests. In this option, you go all in even without experience in retail real estate. Although it can be pretty much uncertain and filled with frustrations, you will realize that any mistakes you make along the way will be very helpful in managing your real estate agency as it grows.

To succeed as a real estate agent, you must master the art of:

#1 Prospecting

#2 Making impressions

#3 Negotiations

#4 Handholding and reassuring clients

#5 Closing a sale

Note: As you do this, it is critical that you master how to leverage on technology to guarantee success.

Chapter 2: The Modern Prospecting: Tapping Into Social Media & Using It As The Ultimate Selling Tool

Often times, it is important to start with the easiest questions first. What is social media anyway? Is it more than just a bloated fad? Social media is what it says it is- an agglomeration of both the social and the media: a marriage of communication and technology where one pretty much helps the other happen or have an elevation in importance (at least in the case of technology). Is social media a fad? To step up your game in the real estate agent world and truly sell in volume, you must dip into and make the social media world part of your own. Approaching it as a fad will only hurt you and your ambitions.

How do you use social media to make your mark as a real estate agent? Here is how: you have to understand and employ extensively all the 5 facets of social media. These are blogging, podcasting, online video, social networking and wikis. In essence, it will be unlikely that you will need to apply each one of these 5 to truly reach mainstream success. In addition to understanding the above categories and applying any one of choice, here are several things you will be wise to take up and do to succeed and sell consistently.

Whether you choose to blog, put out podcasts in plenty or do the occasional podcast video, it will do you a lot of good to:

Consistently post about your neighborhood

Do not be shy showing off your neighborhood listings. This will not only market your area to any prospective residents there may be, but also it will broadcast your passion and knowledge of the homes you are selling and where you are selling them. For instance, if there happens to be a new community center up for sale, then by all means post about it. Express not just the merits that this community center is apt to have tagged to it, but how it is bound to make the lifestyles of the residents more improved. Post about how the center is bound to affect the lives of new residents and stress about how it will likely be an upgrade to anything the resident had at his disposal in his previous place. Of course, it will be important to go by facts.

Every time you update your stuff, use images

They say that a picture is worth 1000 words, and that is just in the casual life. How much more of an impact do you think images will have where real estate is concerned? For instance, pick Facebook- the images there have to be the most engaging content type on the platform. The more likes, comments and shares your post gets, the more they are likely to be viewed in news feeds by the friends of your Facebook fans. Who are the fans? These are the people that like your Facebook page. You can bet that number will increase if your posts are popular with your existing fan base.

Do what most real estate agents do and post extensively about events, especially those in your neighborhood

Events broadcast market the culture of a place. Do you know the leading reason why most people travel, be it to reside in a place or just for tourism? Well, the answer is the potent draw of a place's culture. When you post on the events of your neighborhood, you have the chance to show off just how awesome the city culture of your neighborhood is. Do not be selective either; post about those nondescript, local events that are going down in your neighborhood. If you happen to be venturing out for a neighborly event, how about you post about it and invite your fans to join you in having a good time? To spark and amplify some good old engagement, ask questions to your followers. Nothing beats a question in engaging souls and triggering involvement.

Set up contest to engage potential clients

Regardless of whether you are blogging, podcasting, posting online videos, going the wiki way or networking socially, sweepstakes and contests will provide a phenomenal platform to create and enhance not just engagement, but traffic your way. What is more, it opens up a fun tap that is often very absent where real estate matters are concerned. There is no cap on the types of contests you can set up to deepen the customer-client relationship - just go for it. Contests will be very helpful in promoting you as a realtor who fits the mold of a professional and yet, is able to go about things different. If it interests you, feel free to use them to market your listings as well.

Are you starved of contest ideas? Start things off with the good old photo contest. You can even use these to get a higher number of images on a listing that is new as well as follow up any clients that have recently renovated.

You need to post your listings consistently and without fail

This will not be hard if you have a social media platform of choice set up and listings present. If any of these two are absent, you are doing a poor job of being a realtor, especially the latter. The gold-coated rule of social media is the 80-20 rule. This means that 80% pertains to customer interests, lifestyles and updates in general while 20% regards your particular product. This works to keep your social media social, which should be the point in the 1st place. It also keeps it engaging while being all about business.

While you are posting your listings, keep your personality as well as the identity of your social media platform (blog, Facebook page, Twitter Handle, podcasts etc.). This is certainly not a print ad. Give information about the home and the selling points that it has to it. Keep things engaging and do not forget to tell the price of the home. You will be looking to get comments about what people like about it so you will need to round your posts off with questions. If there are open houses, ensure to set a post aside for these as well.

Chapter 3: Real Estate Agent Networking: Using This To Broaden Your Customer Base And Bring In The Money

Where real estate agents are involved, technology is a lot more than a tool of convenience; it is a way to broaden circumferences and trigger the landslide that is success. This is why you have to embrace networking, push it via technology and add the toppings of movement and tech literacy. How do you go about real estate agent networking? Here is how to go about successful networking as well as ensure that you are perpetually at the top of the game where the same is concerned.

Networking events

Networking will almost always inevitably bring about networking events, especially if there is real growth. Now, if you really want to know where the serious client base resides, look no further than paid networks. People only fork out their money when they are serious about something. Paid networking is almost always better than the unpaid kind, especially where events are concerned. The truth is that in most instances, unpaid networks attract broke agents trying too hard to sell to people who are not fully decided on real estate. So in many instances, the only fellows affiliated to these that will make money are the debt counselors.

Take the initiative & follow up your contacts

Certainly, you will want to pick up mobile phone numbers to boost the likelihood of potential customers becoming actual customers. Pick up contacts and take the initiative of being the first one to place the call. Keep it simple and free of frills: just give them a call and ask for permission to keep in touch. This is all that you are going to need when you are making those all important first steps.

Make use of contact management programs

Have you heard of Market Leader? It is a supremely useful contact management program. Enter every contact you pick up into your contact management program to streamline your life. Some of these programs will separate your contacts nicely based on whether they are buyers, sellers, or browsers. They will even help you track your business performance, help build relationships and generate new leads with greater ease to increase the number of times you get to close sales.

Just to give you an example, the Market Leader allows you to send property blasts to your contact lists (property blasts are email announcements relating to new listings to contacts who have been searching for something similar). You can even send out MLS listings alerts to prospects depending on your selected criteria, send custom campaigns to individual people and even send customers with relevant neighborhood data that they were searching on your website.

Via all means including making use of technology, create own "events"

Of course, seminars will take up a lot of your time and demand that you put in place a lot of planning procedures. However, rest assured that people will certainly line up after the event to have an exchange with you. The other phenomenal thing is that this crowd that lines up to speak to you will usually be devoid of competing agents.

Have a marketing plan put in place

Failing to plan is planning to fail. We all know that all too well. This simply means that you need a marketing plan to act as your roadmap to your success as a real estate agent. You will use the plan to soften up any new acquaintances between any phone calls that you make. The marketing plan should establish you as someone who is an expert while amplifying your mind-top awareness. If at all you do not have a marketing plan in place, then you are wasting way too much time in your efforts in prospecting. Marketing is the lifeblood of networking- it is what makes networking work. With time, effective networking will lead to effective prospecting.

Take and keep notes: Be a taxman in that regard

Talk to potential customers about their lives and their families and be sure to keep these at the back of your mind. The more that you know about your clients, the better you are able to serve them as their agent. Case in point- if your client is being transferred to another city shortly, they will let you know about it if you take the time and effort to know them. Chances are that they will be listing a house. If you are updated when that will go down, then you can step in and deliver a well-timed phone call.

Chapter 4: Developing That All Important Online Personal Presence Via Technology

Note: The importance of a website in modern day business cannot be overlooked especially if you are a real estate agent. You need a responsive and interactive website that will help you in running your real estate business on "autopilot" since this is where you will list property on sale and do so many other things while establishing yourself as a reputable real estate agent. As you become more popular, you will find it a lot easier to generate new leads through the website, which is a plus for you since you can start spending more time handholding and reassuring your clients. You can as well use this time to know more about the area and gathering other useful knowledge that will give you an edge.

How do you go about creating a potent online presence? To begin with, you have to take care of the fundamentals of creating an online presence before hitting the advanced stages. Keep things spick and span, let your spelling and grammar be flawless and most importantly, keep all of your content professional. Besides taking care of the teething stages, how do you go about creating an online presence that draws the attention of customers everywhere? Here is how:

Be very specific when it comes to your accomplishments

Are the adjectives you use to describe your accomplishments specific? If you have used phrases like "I have extensive experience" or "I am results oriented" and "dynamic", it is unfortunate because that is exactly the choice of words that goes against standing out or being unique. If anything, they make you nondescript. LinkedIn analytics labeled these phrases as the most abused phrases.

Rather than use vague descriptive adjectives that do more than slightly power your online presence, try specificity. Choose words that do not just inform but also describe your skill set comprehensively. If you are both "innovative" and "dynamic", then explain just how you are these things.

Quantify your results

If you have already quantified your results, then take a step back and ponder on what your words actually mean.

Try to quantify your experience as well as accomplishments as you build these up. Have you managed to successfully sell houses to 5 of your clients in the past year? Quantifying results serves to put your ability into context.

Be consistent in updating your material

This not only applies to updating new content but linking the older sales you have made as well so that they add weight to your online presence. As you update content and post about new things, be keen to go back to the older content and link it to the new content you have. The thing you are trying to do here is to increase your chances of broadening your customer base and in the process, growing as an online brand.

Keep yourself aware of cultural meanings

Are you aware of what your choice of words means? Be sure to keep in mind that the internet is international- that's what that "inter" stands for in the first place. It is unlikely that you will have to bury your head too deep in the dictionary as a realtor but still, take care of the words you use and how you use them to avoid being misinterpreted. It is important to keep yourself culturally aware of not just individual words but the varied meanings they may have from place to place.

By all means, get recommendations

Really, you cannot afford to just keep pushing the days without at least having some form of recommendations package working for you. Take the time to request good recommendations from past colleagues and especially, those customers you have had progress of any sort when it comes to the customer-realtor relationship. The reviews should be vocal on the interactive qualities as well as show the complete breadth of what you have accomplished with the client. Having multiple and up to date recommendations from your customers will provide you with an incredible amount of credibility.

Upgrade your photo bank

When was the last time that you upgraded your profile photographs? Regularly update your photographs; the visual appeal will also weigh in favorably for you. Remember you are in real estate agency business and impressions have a profound effect on whether you will generate new leads and close a sale or not.

Chapter 5: Leveraging On Mobile Technology As A Real Estate Agent

Why is mobile technology a vital element when it comes to real estate success?

Think about that famous saying that goes, "If Mohammad won't go up to the mountain, then the mountain will go up to Mohammad". It is the same thing with mobile technology and the client base. The clients, as well as their respective assets are not in your office; they are located outside your office, at least for the most time. To maintain effectiveness and provide the best possible customer service, you need to bring your office right up to them. In essence, what you are doing is calling on them. This does not just point to totting your iPad or laptop along as you drop in on them; it means providing them service in whatever way possible.

Think about it this way, it could well mean allowing your customer base to use the tool of technology in whatever way they feel is convenient to them. For instance, you can well power your customer service experience by placing a contract in the palm of your customer's hand via their tablet or Smartphone. The core thing here is this: never inconvenience your clients during a sales process. Additionally, you need to be totally seamless as you bring technology to your customers in the midst of their busy lives.

Real life example of why mobile technology is vital

One real estate agent who is referred to as a vocal evangelist for technology gave a moving account of why his regard for mobile technology in Real Estate is as deep seated as it is. His female client was moving from her home to a nursing home since she was too old to take care of herself. Her home had to be put up for sale but was put in a trust that had her 7 children as trustees. The hard bit was that all 7 of her children were scattered around in 4 states and were in constant motion all the time. Real Estate documents usually require the combined signatures of trustees, but in this case, it was a little too much to bring all the seven of them to California. Still, the realtor had to produce a cleanly executed document and scans and faxes could not have helped the case. Enter Docusign, and the dilemma was solved in an instant. It took very little time for all 7 to docu-sign the work. What was the major inspiration and what docusign platform did they use? Docusign's mobile platform was what they used.

If it hadn't been for mobile technology, there might have been an awful amount of funds and emotions used up.

Chapter 6: Public Exposure Via Technology

We've all heard of indecent exposure and what it actually stands for. As for decent exposure, well, not so much. But it does exist, and especially in the realtor's world, it is a compulsory necessity if you are to get far in your career and succeed. You may not know this yet, but the average house owner moves about once every 7 years or so, and this is a stat lifted from research conducted by the National Association of Realtors. That said, how do you put yourself out there via technology to ensure that you stay "top-of-the-mind"

Assuming that you now have an online platform set aside in your mind, make friend requests.

This is often labeled a thing for the humble man, but humility almost always seems to precede any vast measure of success. The trouble with most professionals, especially professional realtors, is that they seem to regard forums like LinkedIn as networks for them and their fellow colleagues while Facebook and the rest are places to chew the fat with friends. However, the savvy realtor understands perfectly that Facebook is a realtor's dream through and through. It is unparalleled as a place to constantly update you on the day-to-day activities of the client. Once you are firmly networked with your clients, then it is possible, by a few clicks, to know when they are changing jobs, getting married or welcoming a new baby. Often, these massive events of life usually trigger a move. You are also in a position to post articles pertaining to the housing market, mortgage rates, as well as property listings. Facebook will also help you keep track of birthdays, so you have little excuse not to mail in a card or drop a kind message.

Use Technology (e.g. mobile networking) to make events

Hosting an annual event every passing year will do a lot of good in keeping your visibility high. A good example of an event you can hold is a tick-or-treat stop in front of a home that you are selling. You can even host an Easter egg hunt when April rolls around or perhaps, a neighborhood community service oriented project. If you create positive experiences for your clients, you are adding to the reasons why they would want to call you and keep doing so.

Learn how to "pack things up" for the client

One real estate agent discovered that since she was in the moving industry (as every realtor is), it would do her clients a lot of good to brand items for them to help them move. She personalized moving tape with her corporation logo, her full name, and the company number. What she used to do was give the tape to somebody when they started looking at houses. When the client eventually settled on a house of choice, she would give more tape to him. This is pure genius, as inadvertently, others would view the tape and ask questions, which would eventually lead them to keeping memory of the realtor. The truth is, that tape made her a lot of business. You do not have to specialize in tape, but it is a pretty good place to start.

Chapter 7: Generating Leads: Self Generation Of Leads For Unparalleled Success As A Realtor

As is the case with every business there is, if you truly want your career as a realtor to take off; if you truly want to make profits and sales in volume, then you require leads. You need many leads to make this a possibility. Nothing happens in Real estate without a lead: no sales, revenue/profits/commissions go down without these. Here is how to generate leads, with the invaluable aid of technology, and drum up the profits and sales.

Viral videos work especially for realtors

Creating a viral video takes no formula: just create a video, post it on YouTube for free as well as your own site (this will be free too since you own your site). If the video goes viral, rest assured you will be happy you took the time to post it in your site once all the "link love" comes flowing in. On video page, suggest an offer for the next video in exchange for an option. Purchase some cheap PPC adverts on Facebook, not for promoting your offer, but purely to promote the video. Most people, especially that lot that uses Facebook, Twitter and the like-minded forums love good entertainment. Thus, make sure that the content you post in your video is 100% "info-tainment"; do not merely teach; rather, teach and entertain in one go.

Don't be lay- leverage your real estate

Some people ignorantly cling to the notion that the jury is still out on the effectiveness of social media in generating sales.

However, even these people cannot argue with the fact that social media is extremely powerful for spreading ideas.

The thing to do is to give your leads the chance to spread your messages for you. Rather than use "likes", tag a share button alongside the video; place a "retweet" icon or any other gizmo of the social kind that the forums use to spread material. You may have to pay for a single lead, but that very lead could lead a traffic of 10 more your way.

Do not wait to "butter up"- Just sell

Once you have leveraged your new lead's ability to pass around your message for you as well as generate more hopefully, tag a test to them. Put on offer (it could be a hard or soft one) in front of your leads right away. Again, you are not looking for just any lead: you are looking for the ones that actually buy. The more of these that buy, the higher the number of leads that you will eventually be able to afford.

Chapter 8: Now What After Generating Leads?

Impressions Management

As I already mentioned, the path to closing any real estate transaction should entail prospecting, making impressions, handholding and reassuring, negotiations and closing. Prospecting without being fully prepared on how you will make impressions is useless because you will eventually lose many prospects that would otherwise have converted into sales.

To make great first impressions, it starts with your grooming, the car you drive, where you agree to meet your clients, your office space etc. Don't overlook these because they determine the type of clients that you are likely to attract. Additionally, when going out to show prospective clients a house that is for sale, ensure the place is spotless clean; make them picture themselves living in the house by making sure that the house looks ready for occupation. Discard all the trash and everything else that might not give out the much-needed impression of a house ready for occupancy. This means cleaning the house and the surroundings, having curtains, having door mats, fixing any broken fixtures, emptying the bins, and getting rid of anything else that any new owner would not want to see (cobwebs etc).

Additionally, even if you are a busy agent with prospective clients calling every minute, show your new client that you value them by being 100% present. You might have to switch off your phone during the meeting to ensure you are not being disturbed.

Handholding And Reassurance

So, what happens when something seems not to be going according to plan as the deal progresses? When a client has placed a bid, it is crucial to keep in touch whether there is a counter offer or not. Put yourself in your clients' shoes; would you stay put when someone doesn't contact you or seems to be changing goalposts after you have placed your bid? I am certain that no one would. This makes it very crucial to keep in touch so that you can handhold and reassure the customer that everything is okay and that he or she should give you some more time to get things done. Inform the client even if something goes wrong in the deal. For instance, if the seller's agent has been unable to contact the seller to present the bid within the expected duration, you need to tell your client about it; don't just keep him/her in the dark.

The Art Of Negotiation

If you are successful at handholding and reassuring the client, you need to master how to negotiate and close the deal by making a sale. Many real estate agents do all the above but fail to actually make the sale. You can only count your successes as a real estate agent depending on the number of successful sales you've made. So how do you negotiate and close the sale?

#Use home inspection reports as your negotiation tool

When the home inspection reports come with items than need repairs, you can certainly use that as a negotiating tool to get the price reduced. It is best to advise your buyer that they should quote the price fairly high then help them negotiate the price down using the costs that need to be incurred for home repairs.

Use data as your negotiation tool; not opinion

Although it is just fine to give an opinion when negotiating, it is critical that you use more of data to put your points across. This will ensure that you come out as a credible and knowledgeable person in the industry.

Work with deadlines to your advantage

If a listing is close to expiry, you can bet that this is a great time to negotiate. This is especially because sellers want to see progress in their listing, which means that they are likely to be more open to negotiations compared to if negotiating at the beginning of the listing when they believe that they have more options.

Have a counter offer in place

Don't just negotiate; you also need to have a counter offer in place. And in doing so, you can accompany this with some incentives for the seller to make him or her want to sell the property through you.

Know the sentimental value

Asking the right questions to the seller is likely to bring out some things that the seller holds dear to him or her. This can act as a good negotiating tool since you can know what is important to him or her as you negotiate. Pricing and house ownership is not always about money so be keen to ensure that you understand what it is that makes them tick.

You also need to be aware that money negotiations are really a zero sum game, which means no one should feel that they are getting less value than what they are giving. Your job as a real estate agent is to discover what each party holds valuable and strike a balance between the two. As a rule in business, the party who is most desperate loses so don't show that desperation in your negotiations otherwise you will end up getting less than what you are giving.

#Practice some mindfulness

Selling real estate involves emotions during the negotiations. As such, you need to take the emotions of those who are involved into consideration throughout the transaction. Sellers feel trapped and powerless while buyers feel fearful and reluctant about purchasing a home, which may in turn lose value while others may be thinking that by committing, they might lose out on a better deal at a better price.

It is your job as a real estate agent to make everyone feel happy and comfortable throughout the process if you really want to close the sale.

Note: Ultimately, when handling any real estate transaction, keep in mind that it isn't your money or talking that is going to close the deal. What is most important isn't your convincing and negotiating skills. What is most important in any transaction is to make a buyer like what you are selling and make them feel comfortable about the entire process. Everything else will flow so smoothly that you will be amazed by how easy it is to sell real estate. This means your clients need to have great confidence and trust in your ability to represent their interests throughout the transaction. As such, don't overlook the importance of exceptional customer service coupled with communication and close contact with your clients (past and present) throughout the transactions.

Conclusion

Delving into, and selling real estate be it by use of technology as the main platform or otherwise is a broad topic and it comes with multiple subtopics that often differ greatly from each other.

After you have set specific goals, selected a strategy to go with, acquired valuable knowledge on that particular strategy that will come in handy as a realtor and having extensive talks with a mentor of choice, the next step is to make that first sale. All the scheming and preparation in the world is useless if you do not follow up with action. Ultimately, a realtor's job is to sell, not to endlessly get prepared.

Thank you again for downloading this book!

I hope this book was able to help you to learn how to sell real estate with great ease.

The next step is to implement what you have learnt in this book.

Finally, if you enjoyed this book, would you be kind enough to leave a review for this book on Amazon?

Thank you and lots of good luck to you!